Clever dog!

First published in Great Britain in 2009 by

Quercus
21 Bloomsbury Square
London
WC1A 2NS

Copyright © Quercus Publishing Plc 2009

A CIP catalogue record for this book is available from the British Library

ISBN 978 1 84866 022 9

Printed and bound in China

10 9 8 7 6 5 4 3 2 1

Layout, picture research and authoring by Pikaia Imaging

Clever dog!

Quercus

Look before you leap

Time flies
when you're
having fun

They also serve who only stand and wait

They
are also
weighed,
who only
stand and
serve

It's what is
inside that
counts

Size isn't everything

If you want to get ahead, get a hat

Travel broadens the mind

A journey of
a thousand
miles begins
with a single
step

Don't bite off more than you can chew

Laugh and the world laughs with you

Clothes
maketh
the dog

Good fences make good neighbours

The bigger they are, the harder they fall

Youth is wasted on the young

Life is full
of ups and
downs

On a clear
day you can
see forever

What you
lose on the
swings you
gain on the
roundabouts

Put your best paw forward

Many
hands
make light
work

Beauty is in the eye of the beholder

Two heads
are better

than one

Maybe
tomorrow
I'll wanna
settle down

Love me, love my human

You can't have too many dogs

Home is where the heart is

My home is

my castle

Birds of a feather stick together

warm heart

Things will
soon be
looking up

Sometimes we can't see the wood for the trees

The grass
is always
greener

on the
other side
of the fence

The eyes
are the
windows of
the soul

Keep your friends close

Tomorrow is another day

Not everything in life is black and white

Always follow your nose

Iron bars do not a prison make

Sorry is
often the

hardest word

Nobody likes a backseat driver

Fools rush in where angels fear to tread

Walls have ears

Possession is nine-tenths of the law

ALL PETS MUST BE ON A LEASH

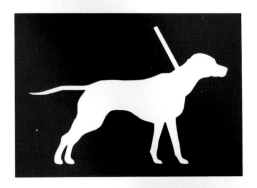

PLEASE CLEAN UP AFTER YOUR PET

PET WASTE TRANSMITS DISEASE

Rules are made to be broken

A friend in need is a friend indeed

Keep your ear to the ground

Always look on the bright side

A good
meal stays
with you

You're only
young once

Good things come in small packages

Chains cannot bind me

You're only
as old as
you feel

The family that plays together,

stays
together

Always
keep your
head above
water

Cleanliness
is next to
dogliness

A dalmatian never changes its spots

Don't worry
Be happy

A rolling stone gathers no moss

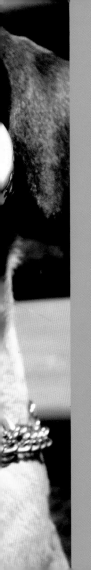

There's always someone cooler than you

Barking dogs seldom bite

Hold on
to what
you've got

Get yourself
connected

Dress
for the
occasion

Now is
the winter
of our
discontent

Tongues will wag

Keep your life firmly on track

Old dog –
new tricks

A healthy mind in a healthy body

What is
this life if,
full of care,
we have no
time to
stand and
stare?

Worrying
never solved
anything

Don't
cry wolf

An hour's sleep before midnight is worth two hours after

Because it's there

Life's a drag

Work, rest

and play

You can't
look into
the future

Why keep a dog and bark yourself?

Keep
young and
beautiful,
if you want
to be loved

First
impressions
last

He who
hesitates
is lost

Let sleeping
dogs lie

Learn to handle your drink

Always take
the high
ground

Look after
number one

Any port in
a storm

It's always
darkest
before
the dawn

Great oaks
from little
acorns grow

Take the road less travelled

Age has its rewards

Stay
informed

Dignity is everything

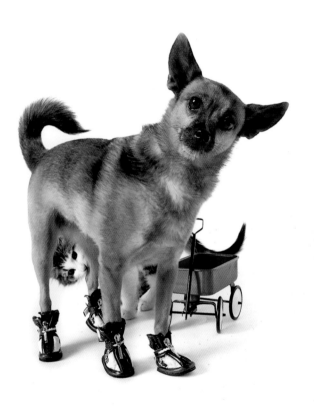

You scratch
my back and

I'll scratch

yours

Every dog
has its day

There is
safety in
numbers

Don't let the
sun go down
on your anger

Stand up and be counted

You can
run but you
can't hide

Jaw-jaw is
better than
war-war

You can't have too much of a good thing

Many
hands

make light
work

Teach your children well

Knowledge
is power

Money
makes the
world go
round

Smiling is infectious

Keep your
mind
active

Go in
with both
eyes open

Live a
good and
useful life

You can't take it with you

Coughs and sneezes

spread
diseases

Eat
yourself
fitter

Don't look a
gift horse

in the
mouth

Don't be
a big head